Immigration to the United States

Chinese Immigrants

Michael Teitelbaum

Robert Asher, Ph.D., General Editor

☑®

Facts On File, Inc.

Immigration to the United States: Chinese Immigrants

Facts On File, Inc.
132 West 31st Street
New York NY 10001

Library of Congress Cataloging-in-Publication Data
Teitelbaum, Michael.
    Chinese immigrants / Michael Teitelbaum.
        p. cm. – (Immigration to the United States)
    Includes bibliographical references and index.
    ISBN 0-8160-5687-0
    1. Chinese Americans–History–Juvenile literature. 2. Immigrants–United States–History–Juvenile literature. 3. Chinese Americans–Juvenile literature. I. Title. II. Series.
    E184.C5T45 2005
    304.8'73051–dc22

                                                                2004014301

Facts On File books are available at special discounts when purchased in bulk quantities for businesses, associations, institutions, or sales promotions. Please call our Special Sales Department in New York at (212) 967-8800 or (800) 322-8755.

You can find Facts On File on the World Wide Web at http://www.factsonfile.com

Cover design by Cathy Rincon
A Creative Media Applications Production
Interior design: Fabia Wargin & Luís Leon
Editor: Laura Walsh
Copy editor: Laurie Lieb
Photo researcher: Jennifer Bright

Photo Credits:
p. 1 © CORBIS; p. 4 © CORBIS; p. 11 © Getty Images/Hulton Archive; p. 15 © Bettmann/CORBIS; p. 20 © Getty Images/Hulton Archive; p. 19 © Getty Images/Hulton Archive; p. 23 © Bettmann/CORBIS; p. 26 © CORBIS; p. 32 © Bettmann/CORBIS; p. 37 © CORBIS; p. 39 © Bettmann/CORBIS; p. 43 © Bettmann/CORBIS; p. 45 © CORBIS; p. 47 Library of Congress/America Memory Collection; p. 48 © CORBIS; p. 51 Library of Congress/America Memory Collection; p. 57 © Bettmann/CORBIS; p. 59 © Bettmann/CORBIS; p. 63 © Charles Jean Marc/CORBIS SYGMA; p. 64 © Time Life Pictures/Getty Images; p. 67 © Associated Press Photo; p. 69 © Bettmann/CORBIS; p. 71 © Alain Nogues/CORBIS SYGMA; p. 72 © Associated Press Photo; p. 74 © Associated Press Photo; p. 77 © Tom & Dee Ann McCarthy/CORBIS; p. 80 © AP Photo/Ira Schwartz; p. 82 © CORBIS SYGMA; p. 84 © Peter Turnley/CORBIS; p. 87 © Reuters/CORBIS

Printed in the United States of America

VH PKG 10 9 8 7 6 5 4 3 2 1

This book is printed on acid-free paper.

Previous page: Two girls wearing traditional Chinese clothes cross a street in the Chinatown district of San Francisco, California.

Contents

A Nation of Immigrants

Robert Asher, Ph.D.

Left: *Chinese immigrant men gather on a San Francisco street in 1901 to hear news of the Boxer Rebellion in their native land.*

Human beings have always moved from one place to another. Sometimes they have sought territory with more food or better economic conditions. Sometimes they have moved to escape poverty or been forced to flee from invaders who have taken over their territory. When people leave one country or region to settle in another, their movement is called emigration. When people come into a new country or region to settle, it is called immigration. The new arrivals are called immigrants.

People move from their home country to settle in a new land for two underlying reasons. The first reason is that negative conditions in their native land push them to leave. These are called "push factors." People are pushed to emigrate from their native land or region by such things as poverty, religious persecution, or political oppression.

The second reason that people emigrate is that positive conditions in the new country pull them to the new land. These are called "pull factors." People immigrate to new countries seeking opportunities that do not exist in their native country. Push and pull factors often work together. People leave poor conditions in one country seeking better conditions in another.

Sometimes people are forced to flee their homeland because of extreme hardship, war, or oppression. These immigrants to new lands are called refugees. During times of war or famine, large groups of refugees may immigrate to new countries in search of better conditions. Refugees have been on the move from the earliest recorded history. Even today, groups of refugees are forced to move from one country to another.

Pulled to America

For hundreds of years, people have been pulled to America seeking freedom and economic opportunity. America has always been a land of immigrants. The original settlers of America emigrated from Asia thousands of years ago. These first Americans were probably following animal herds in search of better hunting grounds. They migrated to America across a land bridge that connected the west coast of North America with Asia. As time passed, they spread throughout North and South America and established complex societies and cultures.

Beginning in the 1500s, a new group of immigrants came to America from Europe. The first European immigrants to America were volunteer sailors and soldiers who were promised rewards for their labor. Once settlements were established, small numbers of immigrants from Spain, Portugal, France, Holland, and England began to arrive. Some were rich, but most were poor. Most of these emigrants had to pay for the expensive ocean voyage from Europe to the Western Hemisphere by promising to work for four to seven years. They were called indentured servants. These emigrants were pushed out of Europe by religious persecution, high land prices, and poverty. They were pulled to America by reports of cheap, fertile land and by the promise of more religious freedom than they had in their homelands.

Many immigrants who arrived in America, however, did not come by choice. Convicts were forcibly transported from England to work in the American colonies. In addition, thousands of African men, women, and children were kidnapped in Africa and forced onto slave ships. They were transported to America and forced to work for European masters. While voluntary emigrants had some choice of which territory they would move to, involuntary immigrants had no choice at all. Slaves were forced to immigrate to America from the 1500s until about 1840. For voluntary immigrants, two things influenced where they settled once they arrived in the United States. First, immigrants usually settled where there were jobs. Second, they often settled in the same places as immigrants who had come before them, especially those who were relatives or who had come from the same village or town in their homeland. This is called chain migration. Immigrants felt more comfortable living among people whose language they understood and whom they might have known in the "old country."

Immigrants often came to America with particular skills that they had learned in their native countries. These included occupations such as carpentry, butchering, jewelry making, metal machining, and farming. Immigrants settled in places where they could find jobs using these skills.

In addition to skills, immigrant groups brought their languages, religions, and customs with them to the new land. Each of these many cultures has made unique contributions to American life. Each group has added to the multicultural society that is America today.

Waves of Immigration

Many immigrant groups came to America in waves. In the early 1800s, economic conditions in Europe were growing harsh. Famine in Ireland led to a massive push of emigration of Irish men and women to the United States. A similar number of

German farmers and urban workers migrated to America. They were attracted by high wages, a growing number of jobs, and low land prices. Starting in 1880, huge numbers of people in southern and eastern Europe, including Italians, Russians, Poles, and Greeks, were facing rising populations and poor economies. To escape these conditions, they chose to immigrate to the United States. In the first 10 years of the 20th century, immigration from Europe was in the millions each year, with a peak of 8 million immigrants in 1910. In the 1930s, thousands of Jewish immigrants fled religious persecution in Nazi Germany and came to America.

Becoming a Legal Immigrant

There were few limits on the number of immigrants that could come to America until 1924. That year, Congress limited immigration to the United States to only 100,000 per year. In 1965, the number of immigrants allowed into the United States each year was raised from 100,000 to 290,000. In 1986, Congress further relaxed immigration rules, especially for immigrants from Cuba and Haiti. The new law allowed 1.5 million legal immigrants to enter the United States in 1990. Since then, more than half a million people have legally immigrated to the United States each year.

Not everyone who wants to immigrate to the United States is allowed to do so. The number of people from other countries who may immigrate to America is determined by a federal law called the Immigration and Naturalization Act (INA). This law was first passed in 1952. It has been amended (changed) many times since then.

Following the terrorist attacks on the World Trade Center in New York City and the Pentagon in Washington, D.C., in 2001, Congress made significant changes in the INA. One important change was to make the agency that administers laws concerning immigrants and other people entering the United States part of the Department of Homeland Security (DHS). The DHS is responsible for protecting the United States from attacks by terrorists. The new immigration agency is called the Citizenship and Immigration Service (CIS). It replaced the previous agency, which was called the Immigration and Naturalization Service (INS).

When noncitizens enter the United States, they must obtain official permission from the government to stay in the country. This permission is called a visa. Visas are issued by the CIS for a specific time period. In order to remain in the country permanently, an immigrant must obtain a permanent resident visa, also called a green card. This document allows a person to live, work, and study in the United States for an unlimited amount of time.

To qualify for a green card, an immigrant must have a sponsor. In most cases, a sponsor is a member of the immigrant's family who is a U.S. citizen or holds a green card. The government sets an annual limit of 226,000 on the number of family members who may be sponsored for permanent residence. In addition, no more than 25,650 immigrants may come from any one country.

In addition to family members, there are two other main avenues to obtaining a green card. A person may be sponsored by a U.S. employer or may enter the Green Card Lottery. An employer may sponsor a person who has unique work qualifications. The Green Card Lottery randomly selects 50,000 winners each year to receive green cards. Applicants for the lottery may be from any country from which immigration is allowed by U.S. law.

However, a green card does not grant an immigrant U.S. citizenship. Many immigrants have chosen to become citizens of the United States. Legal immigrants who have lived in the United States for at least five years and who meet other requirements may apply to become naturalized citizens. Once these immigrants qualify for citizenship, they become full-fledged citizens and have all the rights, privileges, and obligations of other U.S. citizens.

Even with these newer laws, there are always more people who want to immigrate to the United States than are allowed by law. As a result, some people choose to come to the United States illegally. Illegal immigrants do not have permission from the U.S. government to enter the country. Since 1980, the number of illegal immigrants entering the United States, especially from Central and South America, has increased greatly. These illegal immigrants are pushed by poverty in their homelands and pulled by the hope of a better life in the United States. Illegal immigration cannot be exactly measured, but it is believed that between 1 million and 3 million illegal immigrants enter the United States each year.

This series, Immigration to the United States, describes the history of the immigrant groups that have come to the United States. Some came because of the pull of America and the hope of a better life. Others were pushed out of their homelands. Still others were forced to immigrate as slaves. Whatever the reasons for their arrival, each group has a unique story and has made a unique contribution to the American way of life. ❖

Right:
This illustration shows life on a crowded Chinatown street in San Francisco about 1900.

Chinese Immigration

Seeking a Better Life

Chinese immigrants have been coming to the United States in great numbers for more than 150 years. During that time, the new arrivals have been viewed in many different ways by those who were already in the United States. At first, the Chinese were thought to be exotic and mysterious. Few Americans knew anything about China or its people. The early immigrants were welcomed. They were seen as hardworking and productive.

Eventually, though, Chinese immigrants were feared and hated. For 60 years they were barred from coming to America. In more recent times, Chinese immigrants have been admired for the importance many of them place on hard work, family, and education. Many Chinese immigrants have achieved great success in science, technology, music, literature, the media, and other areas. Most have become productive members of American society.

Throughout history, both difficult conditions in China and the lure of a better life in America have led to Chinese immigration. There have been three great waves of Chinese immigration to the United States. The first took place in the early 1850s. Drought, floods, government corruption, high taxes, poverty, and civil wars had led many in China to think about leaving their homes. When gold was discovered in California in 1848, many poor people left China in hopes of striking it rich in America.

More than 20,000 Chinese immigrants came to California seeking gold. Many ended up working as laborers on the transcontinental railroad, which linked the east and west coasts of the United States. This first wave of Chinese immigrants also brought important farming techniques, mining and construction know-how, and a sense of teamwork and cooperation to their new home. Chinese immigrants moved east from California. By the end of the 19th century, "Chinatowns" had developed in cities all across the United States.

Chinese Names

Chinese names are usually made up of three parts. Unlike American names, the first part of a Chinese name is the family name, shared with parents and other relatives. The second part is a generational name. All the children of a particular generation within a family will have the same "middle" name. The third part of a Chinese name is the specific name of an individual child, called the first name or given name in the United States. For example, the Chinese leader Mao Zedong (Mao Tse-Tung) had a three-part name. Mao was his family name. Ze was the name given to the children in his family who were born in his generation. Dong was his given name.

Chinese Language

Within the Chinese language there are many different dialects, or variations in the way it is spoken and written. These dialects vary by region. Each dialect has its own pronunciations, characteristics, symbols, and vocabulary. Some of the most common dialects are Mandarin, Cantonese, Taiwanese, Jin, Wu, Gan, and Jianghuai.

The Chinese written language is made up of individual symbols that each represent one word. This is unlike English, in which each symbol, or letter, represents a sound and words are made of combinations of letters. As a result, Chinese has many more characters than English does. In order to read a Chinese newspaper, a person must understand about 40,000 characters.

When Chinese is translated into English, the word symbols are written phonetically, as they sound. There are two main methods for doing this. The first method is called Wade-Giles. In 1979, a new method called pinyin was adopted by most translators. In most cases, the pinyin and Wade-Giles spellings are not the same.

This book uses pinyin and puts the Wade-Giles spellings in parentheses when a word is used for the first time. In some cases, the pinyin and Wade-Giles spellings are the same so nothing appears in parentheses. In a few instances, some people are so well known by the Wade-Giles version of their names (for example, Chiang Kai-shek) that only that version is used.

Racism and fear led to the Chinese Exclusion Act of 1882, a law passed by the U.S. government that greatly limited Chinese immigration to the United States for 60 years. During World War II (1939–1945), the act was repealed, or ended. When a political group known as the Communists took over the government in China in 1949, the second great wave of Chinese immigration followed. This time, the immigrants were successful, educated Chinese people who fled the tyranny of the new Communist government.

The most recent wave of Chinese immigration took place during the 1980s and 1990s. The relationship between the United States and China, which had been tense, improved during that period. Trade and cultural exchanges led to easier movement between the two countries. A third wave of Chinese immigrants poured into the United States. For those reasons, many Chinese people came to America directly from mainland China. But others came from Hong Kong and Taiwan.

Hong Kong, a city on the coast of China, was a British colony for many years and politically separate from the larger nation of China. It was a place of business and industry. While many Chinese who fled the mainland for freedom when the Communists took over in 1949 went to the United States, some went to Hong Kong. Once they were established in successful businesses there, many took the next step and went to the United States, seeking greater success. The same is true for Taiwan, a small island off the coast of China. Some Taiwanese parents sent their children to the United States for a college education.

Whether they came from mainland China, Hong Kong, or Taiwan, Chinese immigrants brought their culture and traditions to the United States. Immigrants from this ancient country continue to be pulled to America, seeking greater opportunities for themselves and their families. 🔳

Opposite: The Great Wall of China stretches for miles across the landscape in this photo taken about 1900.

Chapter One

Life under
Manchu Rule

An Insulated Society

Behind the Great Wall

China has a long history and a rich culture. It is one of the oldest civilizations in the world. To many Europeans and Americans, China has long been a land of great mystery. Throughout various periods of its history, China's borders were closed to foreigners, adding to this sense of the unknown.

China's 3.7 million square miles (9.6 million km²) of land make it the third-largest country in the world (behind only Russia and Canada). This geographically diverse land contains vast deserts, great river valleys, and some of the world's tallest mountains. China has the largest population of any nation on Earth. More than a billion people, or 20 percent of the world's population, live in China.

China

Perhaps most impressive, though, is that China boasts a civilization that may stretch back as far as 10,000 years. For 5,000 of those years, customs, culture, and traditions remained almost unchanged.

Much of Chinese history is composed of a series of dynasties. A dynasty is a family or ethnic group that rules a country for a period of years. The first recorded dynasty in China was the Shang dynasty, which ended in 1000 B.C. China was ruled by dynasties for thousands of years.

When a group called the Manchus took control of China in the 17th century, the rule of the dynasties was over. And in the centuries that followed, conditions got so bad that by the mid-1800s Chinese people had begun to think of leaving their homes and the land of their ancestors.

The Great Wall of China, begun around 770 B.C., was built over the course of many hundreds of years. The wall stretched for more than 1,000 miles (1,600 km) north of the capital city of Beijing. It was an amazing feat of human engineering and construction. For generations, the Great Wall acted as a defensive shield. It kept out invaders from the north. The wall also became a symbol of power for the emperor.

It's a Fact!

Under Manchu rule, most Chinese people lived in small country villages. They slept on cloth mats on dirt floors and used bamboo pillows or even wooden stools to rest their heads. Some people were so poor they ate tree bark or clay to survive.

Then, in 1644, the Manchus, an ethnic group from an area north of China called Manchuria, invaded China. They battled their way past the Great Wall and overthrew the Ming dynasty. The dynasty the Manchus set up, called the Qing (Ch'ing) dynasty, would be China's last.

Life in China under the Manchus changed greatly. The Manchu rulers cut China off from trade with the outside world.

They told the Chinese people that China possessed everything anyone could possibly need. They said that there was no reason to import (bring in) anything from outsiders.

The Manchus not only stopped foreigners from coming to China, they also made it illegal for Chinese people to leave the country. The leaders of the Qing dynasty worried about their position of power. They feared that anyone leaving China might join forces with outsiders to overthrow the dynasty.

By the year 1800, the population of China had grown to almost 300 million people. While the upper classes were flourishing under Manchu rule, life for Chinese peasants grew more and more unbearable. As in Europe, the rich lived like royalty in museum-like mansions. Just outside these magnificent homes, the poor wallowed in extreme poverty.

The emperor also demanded high taxes from the peasants, which further took away what little they had. The peasants grew hungry, and some starved to death. Some began to talk about seizing land from the wealthy and dividing it among the poor.

Nature was also unkind to the Chinese peasants in the early 1800s. Years without rain parched the land, ruining crops. The Chinese people, forbidden by the government to leave their country, were growing more eager to go elsewhere. They wanted to go anywhere they could make a living and feed their families.

Foreign Trade Resumes

By the middle of the 1800s, after years of pressure from foreign governments, the Manchu rulers in Beijing opened a single port for foreign trade. The port city of Guangzhou (Kuang-chou, or Canton) in the southeastern province (similar to a state) of Guangdong (Kwangtung) became the entry point for foreign goods.

Guangzhou was far from the country's rulers in Beijing. This soon made it the exit point for Chinese emigrants leaving the country against the wishes, and laws, of the Manchu rulers.

Foreign traders faced a big problem in China. The Chinese people were not interested in the products, such as furs, food, and clothing, that the foreigners brought from Europe. The European traders wanted to buy Chinese goods but could not always afford them because they had trouble selling what they had brought to China.

By the early 1800s, however, the British found a solution to this problem. They discovered something that the Chinese people *were* interesting in buying. This was opium. Opium is a powerful, dangerous, and extremely addictive drug. It is made from the poppy, a type of flower. At that time, the poppies were grown in nearby India, a British colony. There, they were processed into opium by a British company under orders from the royal leaders of England.

Confucius

One of the most influential people in Chinese history was the philosopher Confucius. He was born more than 2,000 years ago, but his ideas still influence Chinese people everywhere. His philosophy was based on the importance of duty, harmony, and respect for authority. He believed that if each individual did his or her duty (at school, work, or home), got along with others, and showed proper respect for authority, especially elder family members, then society as a whole would experience peace and prosperity. The rulers of China during Confucius's lifetime, however, did not accept his ideas. Confucius died in 479 B.C. Four hundred years later, his philosophy became the official religion of China, and it still shapes Chinese life today.

Two Chinese men are shown smoking opium about 1865. Smoking mild forms of opium was a common practice among the Chinese people of this time.

Chinese people had been smoking opium for many centuries. However, the opium they had always used was a much milder form of the drug. The opium made in India was so strong that its users quickly became addicted. Upon smoking the drug, the users fell into a comalike state. They neglected their work, their families, and even forgot to eat. They were soon reduced to almost lifeless shells.

The Indian opium brought into China by the British sold quickly. Soon huge profits were flowing back to England. But the drug was swiftly destroying Chinese society, and the Manchu rulers decided to stop its importation. In 1839, the Manchu emperor ordered an end to the flow of opium into China. The British ignored this order. In response, Chinese officials boarded British ships in Guangzhou Harbor and destroyed 20,000 chests–more than 3 million pounds (1.35 million kg)–of opium by burning the drug or dumping it into the sea.

Britain responded quickly and fiercely. It sent its heavily armed navy to invade China. Its goal was to force China to allow it to continue the opium business. The resulting conflict, which lasted from 1839 until 1842, became known as the Opium Wars.

Although the Chinese fought as best as they could, they were no match for the powerful British navy. The Chinese were not equipped to fight sea battles. They did not have huge, heavily armed warships like those the British sent. Britain eventually won the Opium Wars, forcing the Chinese government to sign the Treaty of Nanjing (Nanking) This agreement forced the Chinese to pay Britain for all the opium they had destroyed. It also required them to open five ports in Guangdong province to British traders and to allow the unlimited importation of opium into the country.

Other nations, such as France, Germany, Russia, and the United States, quickly demanded and received the same rights to bring their goods into China. As a result, Chinese people began buying the new foreign goods flowing into the country. Many Chinese merchants began losing money. Poor people had been talking about leaving China for opportunities in other lands for a long time. Now the merchants began to talk about it as well.

Rebellion

By the early 1850s, the desperation of the Chinese peasants finally boiled over into organized rebellions against the Manchu rulers. Manchu soldiers battled the rebellious peasants and the country was plunged into civil war. The Manchu soldiers eventually stopped the rebellion. Then the Manchu government punished the peasants by taxing them or taking away their land. Now their lives were worse than ever.

Around this time, word of instant wealth in a faraway land began to reach China. Tales of unlimited gold, there for the taking, filled the hopes and dreams of Chinese peasants. They called this distant land Gum Shan, which meant "Gold Mountain." In reality, Gold Mountain was California, where, in 1848, gold had been discovered.

This news spread through China, particularly in Guangdong province. Chinese men spoke of taking the long journey to Gold Mountain, making a quick fortune, and returning home with enough wealth to take care of their families.

One Chinese immigrant enticed by Gold Mountain was 14-year-old Huie Kin. He described his decision to leave his home:

> *Once a cousin returned from Gum Shan, the "Gold Mountain," and told us strange tales of men becoming tremendously rich overnight by finding gold in river beds. We knew what poverty meant. To toil and sweat year in and year out, as our parents did, and to get nowhere; to be sick without a doctor's care; going without shoes, even in cold winter days; without books or time to learn to read them—that was the common tale of rural life, as I knew it.*

The first great wave of Chinese immigration to the United States was about to begin. ❖

Opposite: *Chinese men search for gold in a California stream during the gold rush of the mid-1800s.*

Chapter Two

Life on Gold Mountain

Coming to America

The Long Voyage

Word spread of the fortunes to be made on Gold Mountain. More and more Chinese men left their homes and families to take the long journey to California. A few of those who made the journey were well-off enough to pay for their passage across the Pacific Ocean. Most, however, could not afford to pay for the trip. It cost $40 to $60 (about $900 to $1,350 in today's money) to buy a ticket for the four- to eight-week trip from Guangzhou to San Francisco aboard a steamship.

Most Chinese who came to America during the second half of the 19th century paid for their journey in one of two ways. Some came as contract workers. These men agreed to work for a specific number of years for one employer, who paid for the cost of the steamship ticket. Most Chinese contract workers were under contract to other Chinese people who were already in America. The contractors almost always treated their own countrymen horribly, forcing them to work long hours under dangerous conditions and treating them like slaves.

Others came using the credit-ticket system. Under this agreement, a broker, or middleman, paid for the ticket. The traveler would then repay the broker for the cost of the ticket, plus 4 to 8 percent interest, over the next five years.

Conditions on the ocean voyage to America were cramped and dangerous. Travelers slept in tiny bunks stacked less than two feet apart from each other. The below-deck compartments were filthy and overcrowded. The food was poor, and there was little clean water for washing. Disease spread quickly among the tightly packed immigrants in these unsanitary quarters. Nearly 20 percent of the Chinese men who set out from Guangzhou died on the trip across the Pacific. Others suffered from constant seasickness. An article in the August 28, 1888, issue of the *San Francisco*

Examiner newspaper gave a description of the conditions aboard a ship bringing Chinese immigrants to California:

> *It would be a strange sight to one not accustomed to it to see a framework of shelves, not eighteen inches apart, filled with Chinese. If a few barrels of oil were poured into the steerage hold, its occupants would enjoy the distinction so often objected to, of being literally "packed like sardines."*

Despite the difficult journey, the Chinese came by the thousands to seek their fortunes.

The Gold Rush

Before gold was discovered in California in 1848, San Francisco was a small town. It had a population of about 500 people. Early word of the discovery of gold brought a flood of people from the East Coast of the United States. Then came immigrants from Hawaii, South America, Europe, and Mexico. By 1850, San Francisco had grown into city of more than 30,000 people. By the time the Chinese began arriving by the thousands in 1851, San Francisco had become one of the biggest cities in the United States.

New Chinese arrivals wasted no time in joining many others in working the mines of California. Approximately 85 percent of the more than 20,000 Chinese in California by 1852 worked in the mines.

A lucky few found large chunks of gold, giving them instant fortunes. But for most, the dream of quick wealth that had lured them across the ocean did not come true. Some worked for years, living in tents or broken-down cabins. Some spent every hour of the day at the backbreaking work of mining but never found any gold at all.

*Chinese immigrant miners pose for a picture about 1900 along with
African-American and white laborers.*

Many found small amounts of gold. This was enough to
pay for what they needed. It also encouraged the immigrants to
keep looking for gold. Some sent money they had earned back
to their families in China. Others returned to China once they
had earned enough money. Some stayed in the United States
and bought land or businesses.

At first, the Chinese miners were welcomed by those who
had come to California before them. The Chinese quickly developed a reputation as hardworking, quiet, clean, and clever
newcomers. Like most immigrants, they kept to themselves in
crowded groups, working, eating, and living together.

Over time, Chinese miners began buying the rights to mines that were considered worthless and used up by the Americans who had previously worked in them. Often the Chinese miners found additional gold in these supposedly "dried-up" mines.

These miners used special mining techniques developed in China. They dammed up rivers with pine trees. This allowed the miners to control the flow of water so they could use its power to speed up the digging and sifting process.

Another advantage that Chinese miners had over others was their sense of teamwork. Mining during the California gold rush could be dangerous. Miners competed against each other for the best places to dig mines. Violence often broke out when two or more miners wanted to dig in the same area. But instead of competing against each other, Chinese miners would pool their money together in order to buy a mine others had given up on. They would then work the mine as a team and share the profits from any gold they discovered.

As the Chinese grew more successful in the gold mines, white miners began to get angry at them. They were envious of the success of the Chinese. Some white miners even took to violence. They raided Chinese mining camps and beat up Chinese miners. An article in the August 8, 1853, issue of the *San Francisco Alta California* newspaper describes one such act:

> *An American yesterday attacked a Chinaman, beating him shamefully. The Chinamen were afraid to interfere. The assailant [attacker] had the unfortunate Celestial [a name used by Americans of this time to describe Chinese people] by the queue [braid] and kicked and beat him until he was tired.*

It's a Fact!

Many early Chinese immigrants working in the California gold mines replaced their traditional Chinese silk caps and cotton shoes with American cowboy hats and cowboy boots.

In an attempt to calm the white miners and stop the violence, in 1852 the government of California passed the Foreign Miners' Tax. This law said that no Chinese person could work in a mine without paying a monthly fee in gold dust to tax collectors.

Rather than decrease violence against Chinese miners, the Foreign Miners' Tax led to more violence, often committed by the tax collectors themselves. In his diary, one tax collector wrote of his experience with a Chinese miner who resisted the unfair tax collection: "I was sorry to stab the poor creature; but the law makes it necessary to collect the tax; and that's where I get my profit."

This unfair tax was the result of racism. White men in power knew they could take advantage of Chinese miners without getting in trouble. Also, because the Chinese could not speak English, they could not explain to the authorities that they were being cheated.

Queues

When the Manchus took control of China in 1644, Chinese men were forced to wear their hair in a long braid called a queue. The queues were worn to show loyalty to the Manchu leaders. If a man cut off his queue, he would be punished. When the first Chinese immigrants came to the United States, they kept their queues. Most had high hopes of going back to China one day, and they did not want to risk punishment upon their return. These immigrants were often teased about their queues by their fellow miners and railroad workers. Later, racist gangs cut off queues just to keep as trophies. In 1912, when the Manchu dynasty was finally driven from power in China, Chinese men in China and the United States cut off their queues to celebrate.

The First Chinatown

Although most Chinese immigrants arriving in California in the early 1850s lived in mining camps, some lived in the city of San Francisco itself. Like most immigrant groups, the Chinese clustered in one area of the city. This helped them feel more at home in their new country. They were with people who spoke their language and had the same customs. At first, this section of the city was called "little China," "little Canton," or the "Chinese quarter." Eventually, it became known as "Chinatown." By the end of the century, Chinatowns would spring up in cities throughout the United States.

The Chinese who settled in San Francisco's Chinatown made a good living by recognizing what services were needed. They then provided these services for both the city's residents and the miners who traveled into town from the mining camps.

Chinese grocery stores soon opened. They sold familiar foods and supplies for Chinese people in their new home. These goods soon became popular with others in San Francisco as well. Items such as tea, dried meat, fish, poultry, and fresh vegetables were sold. Fresh fish caught by Chinese fishermen in San Francisco Bay were also sold.

Chinese restaurants soon followed in Chinatown. By 1852, 20,000 Chinese immigrants had arrived in California. The restaurants of Chinatown provided familiar food and a connection to home for homesick immigrants. Word of the interesting and exotic foods available in Chinese restaurants soon spread to people of all backgrounds. Residents and sightseers alike visited Chinatown's restaurants. The restaurants ranged from simple, one-room basement businesses feeding hungry miners to luxurious, fancy dining rooms catering to wealthy customers.

Chop Suey

A story from the time of the gold rush tells of a group of white miners who showed up at a Chinatown restaurant just as it was closing. The miners were drunk, hungry, and mean. Wanting to avoid an unpleasant scene, the owner of the restaurant decided to serve the miners. He told his cook to use whatever leftover table scraps he had to create a dinner for the men. Stir-frying bits of meat and vegetables together in a wok (a deep, rounded frying pan), the cook created a dish that the owner called chop suey. In Chinese, *chop suey* means something like "odds and ends." The miners loved this exotic Chinese "delicacy" and spread the word. Soon people were showing up at Chinese restaurants all over San Francisco demanding chop suey. The dish remains on many Chinese menus today.

Other people in Chinatown opened laundries. In those days, washing and ironing was considered "women's work." During the gold rush, however, there were few women in the area to do this work. The mining camps were filled with men who had no desire, after a hard day of backbreaking work in the mines, to wash and iron their own clothes. Seeing this need for laundry workers, some Chinese immigrants in San Francisco's Chinatown opened laundries.

Chinese entrepreneurs, or people who start their own businesses, also opened boardinghouses. Miners stayed in these houses on trips to the city, and sightseers stayed while visiting Chinatown. Other Chinese immigrants started importing businesses. They brought tea, silk, porcelain, and other goods to San Francisco from China to sell.

Ninety percent of the Chinese immigrants of the 19th century were men. San Francisco's Chinatown was largely a community of bachelors, or unmarried men. The men lived together, often crowding into small apartments to save money.

They also socialized together in what little spare time they had. Gambling was a popular activity among the men of Chinatown, as was playing music from their homeland. Many did not know how to read or write. To send letters home to China, they found someone who could write and told the writer what they wanted to say in their letter.

An important part of life in San Francisco's Chinatown was the Chinese associations. These organized groups were started by successful Chinese merchants. They helped new immigrants find jobs, homes, medical care, and loans and even arranged burials when people died. They provided a place for immigrants to gather and enjoy their Chinese culture.

The six most powerful Chinese associations were known as the Six Companies. Later, they named themselves the Chinese Consolidated Benevolent Association. The Six Companies held great power in Chinatown. They settled disputes, offered their members protection, and looked out for the welfare of the Chinese community in San Francisco.

When a new immigrant arrived, for instance, he was met at the dock by a representative of one of the Six Companies, who brought him to Chinatown. One immigrant remembered what he saw when he followed the Six Companies' representative to Chinatown: "Our people were all in their native costume, with queues down their backs, and they kept their stores just as they would do in China, with the entire street front open and groceries and vegetables overflowing on the sidewalks."

Another type of Chinese association was started in Chinatown in the 1850s. Groups called tongs were made up of those who rejected the control and power of the Six Companies. The tongs represented the dark side of Chinese life in America. They were involved with crime and drugs. As Chinatowns sprang up all around the United States, Chinese associations of all types continued to grow in power.

Farming and
the Railroad

By the early 1860s, most of the mines that could be worked by individuals or small groups of miners had been emptied of their gold. The Chinese men who had come to Gold Mountain began to find other ways to make a living. Ancient ideas and techniques brought over from China had helped them to be successful in mining. Now they would prove successful in other occupations as well.

Chinese farmers use foot-power to operate an irrigation machine to pump water into their fields to grow crops.

One such occupation was farming. At that time, the region around the Sacramento River in California was useless swampland covered in water. Working throughout the 1860s, Chinese farm workers used ancient techniques to drain the swampland. They dug ditches and canals to remove the water and built levees and dikes to keep it out. Where the water had been was now rich soil.

Soon, crops such as peanuts, currants, peaches, and raspberries were plentiful. Citrus fruits, such as oranges, grapefruits, lemons, and limes, flourished and quickly became important California crops. The once worthless swampland was now very valuable, thanks to the know-how and effort of the Chinese.

Another way in which the Chinese transformed America by applying ancient knowledge was in the building of America's transcontinental railroad. (*Transcontinental* means "across the continent.") Wealthy, powerful Americans had long dreamed of connecting the east and west coasts of the United States. In 1862, Congress, with the support of President Abraham Lincoln, approved funding for the building of a transcontinental railroad.

Two railroad companies were hired to do the job. The Union Pacific Railroad would start in Omaha, Nebraska, and lay train tracks to the west. The Central Pacific Railroad would start in Sacramento, California, and build east. The plan was for the two sets of tracks to eventually meet at Promontory Point, Utah. This new railroad, connected to other railroads in the East, would create a continuous train track that ran from one coast of the United States to the other. To encourage the companies to work quickly, the first one to reach Promontory Point would receive a bonus payment from the government.

While the Union Pacific's tracks would be built on flat plains, the Central Pacific had much more difficult terrain to pass through. The Central Pacific would have to cut a path through high mountains and across blistering deserts.

A Chinese-American Fruit Farmer

Lue Gim Gong, a Chinese immigrant, was born in Guangzhou in 1860 and came to the United States at the age of 20. He got his start in farming in 1886, working in the private fruit orchards of Frances Burlingame in Massachusetts. Burlingame paid for Lue to take farming classes and encouraged him to experiment with the fruit trees in her family orchard. Later, Burlingame bought Lue an orchard in Florida. There he bred and grew huge currants, peaches that ripened very quickly, and new varieties of raspberries. Perhaps Lue's greatest contribution to American farming came in 1911, when he grew the first orange that would not be ruined by frost. This fruit quickly became the foundation of Florida's huge citrus business.

Charles Crocker, one of the four men who ran the Central Pacific Railroad, began hiring workers to lay track. At first, most of the workers he hired were recently arrived Irish immigrants. The work was difficult, dangerous, slow, and tedious. Workers carved train tunnels through the solid granite rock of the Sierra Nevada, a mountain range. They used only hand drills, gunpowder, picks, and shovels.

Crocker's construction boss, J. H. Strobridge, complained that the workers were often drunk and rowdy. Many left their jobs after getting their first paycheck. After two years, only 50 miles (80 km) of track had been built. Hundreds of miles remained. When Strobridge advertised for 5,000 new workers, only 800 showed up. Most people had heard how difficult the work was.

In 1865, Charles Crocker suggested that the Central Pacific hire Chinese workers. Strobridge refused. "I will not boss Chinese," he said. "I will not be responsible for work done by Chinese laborers. I don't think they could build a railroad."

Strobridge claimed that the Chinese people were too small. He said that most of them were under 5 feet (1.5 m) tall and weighed barely 100 pounds (45 kg). He also said that they were not skilled at building. Crocker reminded Strobridge that the Chinese people had built the largest construction project in the world, the Great Wall of China. If they could build that, Crocker insisted, they could build a railroad.

Strobridge agreed to hire 50 Chinese workers. He started them in jobs such as filling carts with dirt. The Chinese workers did an excellent job. He next gave them picks and shovels and had them work on cutting through the mountain. They did this work faster and better than the white workers had.

Within months, 3,000 Chinese laborers had been hired to build the Central Pacific section of the railroad. Men from the Central Pacific were sent to the mines to lure away Chinese workers. Notices were sent to San Francisco and even to China advertising the need for more laborers. Eventually, more than 10,000 Chinese laborers worked for the Central Pacific Railroad.

Chinese workers were paid $35 per month, the same as the white workers. However, the Chinese workers had to pay for their own food and housing, while white workers did not. The Chinese laborers were organized into 12-man teams, including a cook and a leader. The leader reported to the company foreman, or boss.

The cooks made special meals for the Chinese workers. Because they paid for their own food, they were able to eat foods that were familiar to them. These included dried oysters, cuttlefish,

It's a Fact!

A Chinese immigrant named Lalu Nathoy married Charlie Bemis, a saloon owner in Idaho, in the 1870s, and changed her name to Polly Bemis. Her knowledge of Chinese herbal medicine led her to become one of the most respected healers on the western frontier, where doctors were scarce.

abalone, bamboo sprouts, rice, dried fruits, and many vegetables. The Chinese workers drank hot tea rather than cold water. (Boiling the water for tea killed any germs in the water.) The hot tea and healthy, balanced diet of fish, rice, fruits, and vegetables kept the Chinese in better health than the white workers. White workers were often sick from the dirty water they drank. They ate salted beef and bread with butter that was often spoiled. They also ate few if any vegetables. The better health of the Chinese railroad workers was another reason that they were generally more successful at railroad building than their white coworkers were.

The Chinese workers also knew a lot about using gunpowder and explosives. Chinese people had used these skills in their native land for centuries to make fireworks and for construction. They were very valuable skills for the railroad workers, who had to blast through the granite mountains of California. Even so, working with explosives was very dangerous. Many Chinese laborers lost their lives in accidents involving explosions.

The Bet

In April 1869, as the tracks of the Central Pacific and the Union Pacific grew closer and closer to each other, a contest was held to see which company could lay the most track in a single day. Charles Crocker bet an official of the Union Pacific $10,000 that his crew would win. Crocker's crew of Chinese workers laid 10 miles (16 km) of track in a single day, beating the Union Pacific crew and setting a single-day record for the most track laid during the building of the transcontinental railroad. Ten miles in one day was a far cry from the 50 miles (80 km) in two years achieved by Crocker's first crew, which had prompted Crocker to hire the Chinese laborers in the first place.

Chinese laborers move rocks to make a path through the mountains for the Central Pacific railroad line.

Leland Stanford, the governor of California and the president of the Central Pacific Railroad, praised the Chinese laborers. He said they were "quiet, peaceable, patient, industrious, and economical." In an 1865 report about the transcontinental railroad, Stanford told U.S. president Andrew Johnson: "Without them [the Chinese] it would be impossible to complete the Western portion of this great national enterprise."

The railroad owners praised the Chinese to the public. On the job, however, they mistreated them. The Chinese worked longer hours and had to pay for their own food and housing. They were often beaten or whipped by their foremen, who treated them like slaves. As they had in the mines, they faced prejudice and racism working on the railroad. The great success of the Chinese railroad workers caused anger among some of the white laborers. Crocker and Strobridge used the work of the Chinese as an example of what could be accomplished. This angered white workers.

Finally, on May 10, 1869, the two railroads met at Promontory Summit, Utah. Before the building of the railroad, it took up to six months to travel across the United States from coast to coast. Now, the journey could be done in six days.

A golden spike was driven into the ground to mark the completion of the railroad. Celebrations were held and a now-famous photograph was taken of the momentous occasion. No Chinese laborers appeared in the photo. Chinese workers were not allowed to attend the celebrations. They were not even mentioned during the ceremonies honoring the men who had built the railroad. It was common at that time for those in power to treat people of other races unfairly. While they were building the railroad, racism prevented the Chinese from getting decent working conditions. After the railroad was completed, these same racist attitudes kept the Chinese from getting credit for all their hard work.

Opposite: *This cartoon from the 1880s makes fun of Chinese immigrants. It shows the fear that many people in America had that Chinese immigrants would take their jobs.*

Chapter Three

The Era of Exclusion

Chinese Immigrants, Keep Out!

A New Wave

W hen the transcontinental railroad was completed in 1869, thousands of Chinese laborers found themselves out of work. With the gold rush over and the railroad done, the Chinese workers needed other ways to make a living.

At this time, the growing Chinese population in America was spurred on by a treaty that had been signed one year earlier. In 1868, the United States and China signed the Burlingame Treaty. This treaty allowed American and Chinese citizens to move freely from one country to the other. Chinese who came to the United States were allowed to stay as "permanent residents," although they were not allowed to become citizens.

The Burlingame Treaty brought a wave of Chinese immigration even greater than that caused by the gold rush. In the years between 1860 and 1880, the Chinese population in America tripled, to about 100,000 people. Again, most of the immigrants came to California. The new arrivals joined those left unemployed by the end of the gold rush and the completion of the railroad in looking for work.

By 1870, white factory workers on the East Coast of the United States had formed labor unions. They began to demand shorter working days, better wages, and safer conditions. When factory owners refused to meet these demands, many workers went on strike.

That year in North Adams, Massachusetts, workers in a shoe factory owned by Calvin Sampson went on strike. In response, Sampson fired all his workers. He tried to hire other workers in the North Adams area, but no one wanted the jobs. People were afraid of going against the union. Sampson happened to read a newspaper article about Chinese workers in a San Francisco shoe factory. The article reported how efficient, hardworking, and reliable they were. Sampson decided to hire Chinese workers from California and bring them to Massachusetts to replace the striking workers he had fired.

Seventy-five Chinese workers traveled cross-country to work in Sampson's factory. The Chinese workers were greeted by an angry mob who threw stones at them and called them "scabs," "strikebreakers," and "rats." They were angry at the Chinese for replacing the striking workers. After all, if Sampson had new workers for his factory, he would not have to meet the demands made by the strikers. The Chinese workers were soon producing more shoes than the former employees had.

Word of this opportunity spread to other Chinese immigrants in California, who were desperate for jobs. Many headed east. Factories and large laundries in New Jersey, Pennsylvania, and other northern states hired Chinese workers. They often replaced striking white workers and were willing to work for lower wages.

This movement east for jobs led to the formation of new Chinatowns in cities like New York; Newark, New Jersey; and Philadelphia. It also led to more and more Chinese immigrants opening their own businesses, such as groceries, restaurants, and laundries, just as they had done in San Francisco.

Anti-Chinese Feelings

In the 1870s, America faced very hard economic times. The country slid into an economic depression. Factories closed, and many thousands of people were out of work. At the same time that jobs were disappearing, the number of people looking for jobs was increasing.

Soldiers who had recently finished fighting in the Civil War (1860–1865) joined the former miners and railroad workers who were out of work. These soldiers returned home expecting to find jobs. But jobs were scarce.

Employers who did have jobs to fill were trying to save money during this period. Often, they hired workers willing to put in long hours for low pay. Many of those workers were Chinese.

An anxious nation looked for somebody to blame for its economic troubles. The Chinese were easy to blame because they were "newcomers" and were a different race. Some white Americans claimed that Chinese people were taking jobs that belonged to "real" Americans. Ironically, many of the people making these claims belonged to other immigrant groups. One of these groups was the Irish, who had not been in the country very long themselves.

Anti-Chinese clubs were formed. At loud, angry meetings, their members accused the Chinese of being unwanted invaders. The clubs claimed that the Chinese were an inferior race who had come to take away white people's jobs, money, and the American way of life. Pressure began to grow on the government to do something about this "problem."

Most of the Chinese in America still lived in San Francisco. As anti-Chinese feelings there got stronger, the city's government passed laws that made life for Chinese people very difficult.

The Sidewalk Ordinance (law) of 1870, for instance, prohibited people from walking on sidewalks while carrying long poles with baskets on the ends. Since this was an important way in which Chinese workers transported everything from vegetables to laundry, this law was clearly aimed at them.

The Cubic Air Ordinance of 1871 required each adult in the city to have at least 500 cubic feet (14 m³) of living space. At this time, many Chinese immigrants lived together in cramped quarters. Although crowded buildings were also common in poor white neighborhoods, the law was much more strictly enforced in Chinatown.

*This cartoon from the late 1800s illustrates the cruel and racist
treatment that many Chinese immigrants had to face in California.*

The Queue Ordinance of 1873 forced all prisoners in city
jails to cut their hair so that it was no more than 1 inch (2.54 cm)
long. Many Chinese immigrant men, still remembering the laws
of the Manchus in China, had kept their long queues. When the
queues were cut by jailers, the Chinese men were humiliated and
afraid of being punished if they ever returned to China.

The Chinese felt powerless to stop these unfair, racist laws
from being passed. In 1870, Congress had declared that no Asian
immigrant could become a citizen. Therefore, the Chinese could
not vote, so they could not elect leaders who would pass laws
that were fairer to the Chinese.

Violence increased as the country's economic problems
worsened. Anti-Chinese gangs attacked Chinese people at
random. Often the police did nothing to stop such violence. In
October 1871, an incident that came to be known as the

Chinese Massacre erupted in Los Angeles. During a battle between two Chinese tongs, a gunshot was fired. A white police officer was accidentally hit. An angry mob of white people screaming "Hang them!" stormed through the streets, pulling Chinese people from their homes. More than twenty Chinese people were murdered—shot or hanged on the spot.

As the 1870s went on, politicians began adding to the anti-Chinese fury. California governor William Irwin announced that there was "an irrepressible conflict between the Chinese and ourselves—between their civilization and ours." In other words, Chinese and white people had differences that could never be overcome.

An Irish immigrant named Denis Kearney became known for his anti-Chinese speeches in San Francisco. With each speech, the crowds listening to him grew larger. Kearney was soon speaking to crowds of thousands of unemployed, desperate people. He blamed the Chinese for taking what few jobs there were away from whites. Saying that Chinatown should be blown up with dynamite, he ended each speech by shouting "The Chinese must go!" This phrase quickly became the battle cry of the anti-Chinese movement.

At a rally in July 1877, an anti-Chinese group began shouting "Let's go for Chinatown!" In response, a mob of 10,000 people charged into Chinatown. They smashed windows, set fire to buildings, and shot Chinese people they saw on the street. The destruction lasted through the night. By morning, the National Guard had been called out to restore order. But there were simply too many rioters, and they could not be stopped. The violence continued for three days. The mob tried to burn down the docks where Chinese immigrants arrived. Rioters fought against firefighters who tried to stop the blaze. Near the end of the third day, troops from the U.S. Navy arrived and the riot finally ended.

As anti-Chinese feeling spread across the country, more new laws were passed that made it harder for Chinese people to find work. State legislatures as well as the United States Congress talked about restricting, or limiting, Chinese immigration. That talk would result in a law that would limit Chinese immigration for the next 60 years.

White citizens attack Chinese-American residents of Denver, Colorado, in a display of the anti-Chinese feeling that was common in many parts of the Unites States during the late 1800s.

The Chinese Exclusion Act

On May 6, 1882, President Chester Arthur signed into law the Chinese Exclusion Act. This new law banned the immigration of Chinese laborers to the United States for a period of 10 years. Only merchants, teachers, students, tourists, and American-born Chinese were allowed to travel from China to the United States. This marked the first time in U.S. history that a group of people was singled out for limited immigration.

The Exclusion Act had an immediate effect on Chinese immigration. In 1881, the year before the act, 40,000 Chinese had come to America. Within a few years of the act's passage, fewer than 50 Chinese people entered the country per year. More laws restricting Chinese immigration soon followed.

In 1888, the Scott Act was passed. This law prevented even legal Chinese immigrants from reentering the United States once they had left. At the time of the act, about 20,000 Chinese workers were back in China visiting family. They were not allowed to reenter the United States.

The 1882 Exclusion Act proved so effective that when it was about to expire in 1892, American workers pressured Congress to extend it. The Geary Act of 1892 extended the exclusion laws for another 10 years. It also forced all alien laborers (those born in other countries) in the United States to register with the government and carry an identification card at all times.

It's a Fact!

During the era of exclusion, some Chinese people tried to sneak into the United States. Among their hiding places were rice bins and coffins on trains coming from Canada and Mexico and boats coming from the Caribbean.

In 1902 the exclusion laws were extended again for two more years. Then, in 1904, they were renewed for an unlimited period of time.

The effects of these laws were dramatic. In 1880, there were about 105,000 Chinese people in the United States. By 1920, that number had dropped to just over 61,000. The fact that Chinese laborers were not allowed to enter the United States caused this great drop in population.

It was necessary for Chinese immigrants to obtain a certificate of residence such as this one in order to live in the United States legally following the Chinese Exclusion Act of 1892.

Paper Sons
and Angel Island

O n April 18, 1906, a massive earthquake hit San Francisco. Buildings collapsed and fire broke out all over the city. Most of Chinatown was reduced to rubble. People's lives were shattered, their belongings lost, and their homes destroyed.

A Chinese immigrant watches as smoke rises from the destruction caused by the 1906 San Francisco earthquake.

The fires also destroyed the city's birth and citizenship records. This proved to be an important event for Chinese people who wanted to come to America. Because the city's records were gone, many Chinese immigrants living in San Francisco claimed to have been born there rather than in China. Without birth records, the government could not prove otherwise.

Anyone born in the United States is automatically a U.S. citizen. As a U.S. citizen, a person is allowed to bring his or her children to the United States, even if they were born in another country. This law was the same in the early 20th century as it is today.

In the years following the 1906 earthquake, many Chinese immigrants in San Francisco falsely claimed to be citizens. They also falsely claimed to have sons in China. Paperwork was drawn up to bring those "sons" to the United States. These documents were then used to bring other children over. Sometimes the "sons" would be the children of relatives or of friends. In other cases, the documents would be sold to young men who wanted to come to America. Young Chinese immigrants who came over in this way were called "paper sons."

During this time, when Chinese immigrants arrived on the dock in San Francisco, they were held in a small, wooden shed with no windows. It was a cramped, dirty building, where the immigrants were forced to wait for weeks or months before they were interviewed by immigration inspectors.

With the arrival of so many paper sons, a new immigration facility was needed. In 1910, a new immigrant processing center was built on Angel Island, a small island in San Francisco Bay. For the next 30 years, immigrants from many countries, including about 175,000 Chinese, passed through Angel Island before being allowed into the United States.

Most immigrants from other nations were held on Angel Island for a few hours, then allowed into the country. When the

U.S. government learned of the Chinese paper sons with their false documents, it held new Chinese arrivals for a long time. Chinese immigrants often spent months, and even years, on Angel Island. They were asked many questions to see if they really were the sons of citizens.

Hoping to catch a paper son in a lie, an immigration official would ask him very specific questions, such as "How many steps are there in your father's house in China?" "What is your bedroom floor made out of?" "What is your neighbor's name?" and "What kind of chickens does your neighbor have?" The official would then ask the same questions of the man claiming to be the paper son's father. If the answers did not match exactly, the paper son would be sent back to China. Often the paper sons were coached before they left China on the types of questions they might be asked on Angel Island. They memorized tiny details of their homes and villages in order to pass the test.

Although the facility there was new, the conditions on Angel Island were not much better than those in the old shed on the docks. Each immigrant had to strip naked and undergo a physical examination. Often women were examined by male doctors, causing them great humiliation. Helen Wong Hom, who came to the United States at the age of seven with her mother and brother in 1928, wrote of her examination, "The inspectors undressed me because they couldn't believe I was a girl. They thought I was a boy. Mommy didn't like that at all. Chinese are very modest about their bodies, you know."

Men and women were kept in separate buildings. The bathrooms offered no privacy. They contained simply a row of toilets with no stalls. Some Chinese women looked out for each other's privacy by covering their faces with paper bags before going into the bathroom.

In the matter of the
identification of
PON DOO CHEW,
merchant's minor son.
Student and traveler
for curiosity and
pleasure.

Prior landing:- No. 14517/12-16,
ex ss "Manchuria" July 20,1915.

State of California)
City and County of)ss
San Francisco   )

Photograph of
PON DOO CHEW

Pon Doo Chew, being first duly sworn upon oath,
according to law, doth depose and say:-

That affiant is a resident Chinese person, lawfully
domiciled within the United States, having arrived at the Port
of San Francisco, on the ss "Manchuria", on the 20th day of July,
1915, No. 14517/12-16, and after due and proper investigation
affiant was permitted to enter the United States, your affiant
being the minor son of a resident Chinese merchant lawfully
domiciled therein.

That your affiant's father is Pon Hing, a resident
Chinese merchant lawfully domiciled within the United States.
That the said Pon Hing is now, and has been for more than a
year prior to the date hereof, a merchant and member of the firm
of Mow Lee and Co., which is a firm engaged in buying and
selling merchandise at a fixed place of business, to wit:- at No.
720 Grant Avenue, San Francisco, during which time he has engaged
in the performance of no manual labor except such as was necessary
in the conduct of his business, and that your affiant has lived
with his said father since his entry into the United States,
as aforesaid.

That shortly after the landing of your affiant
in the United States he became a student in the Oriental
Public School, at San Francisco, where he remained a student
until just prior to the present time, when he was making
arrangements to go to China upon a temporary visit as
a traveler for curiosity and pleasure, and to visit his
mother and relatives in China, and that this affidavit is
made to facilitate in establishing the identity of your
affiant as such merchant's minor son, student and traveler
for curiosity and pleasure.

*This document identified Pon Doo Chew as a Chinese-American
student who was traveling to China to visit relatives in 1915.
Without it, he would have difficulty reentering the United States.*

The men and women on Angel Island ate at different times,
so that even husbands and wives did not get to see each other.
There was nothing for the immigrants to do but wait to be
allowed into the country. The men gambled and the women

knitted to pass the time. An immigrant named Mr. Lowe, who arrived at Angel Island in 1939 at the age of 16, wrote: "I had nothing to do there. During the day, we stared at the scenery beyond the barbed wires—the sea and the sky and clouds that were separated from us. Some, due to faulty responses during the interrogation [questioning] process, had been there for years."

The Chinese held at Angel Island were treated like prisoners in a jail. Some grew depressed and even committed suicide. Others poured their sorrow and anger into poems, which they carved onto the walls at Angel Island.

Many paper sons did make it into the United States. As the "sons" of citizens, they too became U.S. citizens. As citizens, they were allowed to bring their wives over from China. In the years from 1910 to 1924, more than 1,000 Chinese women came to America this way each year.

It's a Fact!

In 1900, in San Francisco, a Chinese immigrant named Ng Poon Chew started the first daily Chinese-language newspaper in America. It was called *Chung Sai Yat Po,* which means "China West Daily."

This great influx of women greatly changed life in America's Chinatowns. Once mainly bachelor communities, Chinatowns became places for families. A great many Chinese immigrants had children in the United States in the early part of the 20th century. These American-born Chinese are known as second-generation Chinese Americans.

As the numbers of Chinese in America began to grow, a new law once again restricted their flow into the country. The Immigration Act of 1924 prohibited Chinese women (except the wives of merchants, teachers, students, and tourists) from entering the United States. Again, the number of Chinese immigrants coming to America dropped. It would be another 20 years before Chinese women could freely enter the country again.

The Poems of Angel Island

Mr. Ng, who arrived at Angel Island in 1931 at the age of 15, wrote, "The people at Angel Island wrote poems all over the walls, wherever the hand could reach, even in the bathroom. Some were carved, but most were written with ink."

When the Angel Island Immigration Station was abandoned in 1940, the damp, foggy weather of San Francisco Bay destroyed the poems that were written in ink on painted walls. The dampness made the paint flake away. The poems carved into wooden walls survived. They have been preserved as a Chinese-American cultural treasure. Here are a few examples translated into English:

The insects chirp outside the four walls.
The inmates often sigh.
Thinking of affairs back home,
Unconscious tears wet my lapel.

America has power, but not justice.
In prison, we were victimized as if we were guilty.
Given no opportunity to explain, it was really brutal.
I bow my head in reflection but there is nothing I can do.

Why do I have to sit in jail?
It is only because my country is weak and my family is poor.
My parents wait at the door in vain for news;
My wife and child wrap themselves in their quilt,
sighing with loneliness.
Even should I be allowed to enter this country,
When can I make enough to return to China with wealth?

From this moment on, we say goodbye to this house,
My fellow countrymen here are rejoicing like me.
Say not that everything is western styled,
Even if it were built with jade, it has turned into a cage.

Struggles in America

Life for Chinese Americans in the early part of the 20th century continued to be a struggle. During the period of limited Chinese immigration, those who were already in the United States were caught between two tough situations. Many white Americans still refused to accept them, but there was little opportunity to make a living back in China.

Although some worked as farmers in rural areas, most Chinese Americans still lived in cities. Most of those lived in Chinatowns. Restaurants, laundries, and grocery stores still provided a living for many. The Chinese who lived in Chinatowns depended on white American customers, but they maintained their own cultural identity.

By the 1930s, some Chinatowns had existed for more than 50 years. Several generations had grown up there. Chinese holidays and festivals were celebrated regularly. They are still celebrated in almost exactly the same way today.

The biggest celebration of the year was Chinese New Year. This holiday fell in late January or early February. The date was determined by the lunar calendar, which is based on the phases of the moon. As the holiday approached, houses were cleaned and decorated with red paper, which represents good luck.

A huge festival and parade were held in Chinatowns across America to celebrate the new year. A long line of people dressed in a huge paper dragon costume wound through the streets. The dragon was there to chase away evil spirits. Firecrackers and pounding drums filled the air, and streaming paper flooded the streets, also to frighten away evil spirits and usher in luck for the new year.

In Chinese homes, families created huge feasts and exchanged gifts, including lucky red envelopes containing money. Louise Leung Larson, who grew up in Los Angeles in the early 1900s, wrote of her family's celebration:

> *Papa would start preparations several months in advance by planting Chinese lily bulbs in blue planters. They always seemed to bloom just in time for the New Year, and their sweet fragrance filled the house. Mama would get out the special New Year tablecloth, a red silk embroidered cloth with little glass inserts. On the table were sweets such as candied ginger, coconut strips, lichee nuts, and sweet and sour plums. The traditional New Year dish was* tsai, *an assortment of vegetables such as hair seaweed, bean threads, snow peas, bamboo shoots, mushrooms, and cloud ears fungus [mushrooms]. Visitors would come and put* lai see *[money in lucky red envelopes] onto the table. I would say* Gong hay fat choy *[Happy New Year] to each visitor.*

In April, the Ching-Ming Festival was celebrated. Families went together to the graves of family members or close friends. They brought food, lit firecrackers, and burned paper money. The firecrackers were lit to scare off evil spirits. The food and money were offered to ensure a safe journey into the next world for the deceased loved one. This belief was part of the Buddhist religion, which was, and is, practiced by many Chinese.

The third major celebration of the year was the Harvest Moon Festival. It was held in late September or early October. Like the American tradition of Thanksgiving, the Harvest Moon Festival was a time when families gathered to celebrate the harvest and give thanks. The Chinese also honored dead relatives, a long-standing tradition. People ate moon cakes, filled with black beans and lotus seeds, as the full moon shone brilliantly in the sky.

Traditional Chinese arts also thrived in Chinatowns. In Chinatown theaters, groups of traveling performers put on Chinese operas. These plays were often parts of long continuing tales, like modern-day soap operas. They were accompanied by music played on flutes, drums, and cymbals. They lasted for many hours, and most people brought food with them to the theater to snack on.

Eileen Lee recalled going to see a Chinese opera in New York City's Chinatown in the 1920s: "Going to the Chinese Opera at Sun Sing theater was a real treat for me when I was a little girl. My Mom would pack a snack basket. What I remember most was all the colors of the costumes they wore. Another thing I remember is my grandmother telling me that the man on stage was really a woman actress."

Traditional Chinese culture was alive in Chinatowns throughout America. But the image of Chinese people presented in the mainstream American media was very different. Movies, books, and radio programs in the 1920s and 1930s showed stereotyped images of Chinese people. Chinese men were portrayed as mysterious and dangerous or as clownish fools. Chinese women were shown as either delicate China dolls or evil "dragon ladies," who were cunning and ambitious.

In the 1930s, the United States fell into the worst economic depression in its history. The Great Depression, as it became known, did not affect Chinese Americans as badly as the depression of the 1870s had. By the 1930s, Chinatowns were self-sufficient, meaning that they contained everything their residents needed. Therefore, they were somewhat safe from the bad times faced by the rest of the country.

The fact that many Chinese did not trust American banks also prevented them from suffering during the Great Depression. Many American banks failed during the depression because they did not have enough money. Since many Chinese immigrants did not rely on banks and usually borrowed the money they needed from relatives, they did not lose their money during the Great Depression as so many other Americans did.

Lights, Camera, Action

Many people in the film industry feel that James Wong Howe was one of the greatest cameramen ever to make movies. As the person who looks through the camera, the cameraman decides exactly what the audience will see and also chooses the lighting used for each scene. Howe was born in China in 1899. A few years later, his father brought the family to the United States and opened a restaurant in Paso, Washington. In 1916, James Wong Howe got his first job in the motion picture business in Los Angeles, helping famous director Cecil B. DeMille. Howe saved his money and bought a camera. Soon he began experimenting with different lenses and types of lighting. In 1927, he shot and produced his own movie, called *Transatlantic*. It was a success, and soon Howe was in demand as a cameraman. During his long career in Hollywood, James Wong Howe received 16 Oscar nominations. He won two Academy Awards, for *The Rose Tattoo* in 1956 and *Hud* in 1963. Howe died in 1976, but film students still study his work to learn the art of photographing a movie.

On the other hand, Chinese Americans whose businesses, such as restaurants and laundries, provided services to other Americans were affected by the depression. Many Americans of all races did not have jobs, and they could no longer afford these services. As a result, the Chinese business owners did not make as much money as they had earlier.

While the United States struggled with the Great Depression, there was trouble in the Chinese immigrants' homeland. In 1931, Japan invaded China. Chinese Americans followed the events with great anxiety. By 1938, the Japanese army had taken over several coastal Chinese cities, as well as much of northern and central China. It had killed tens of thousands of people in the process.

By 1941, the south of China was occupied by the Japanese army. This area included Guangdong province, from which most Chinese immigrants had come. In the Chinese-American community, letters from home and news of relatives in China became more and more rare. Chinatown grocery stores became centers where people gathered to share what little news they had of the war back home.

As 1941 drew to a close, an event took place that had a huge effect on Chinese immigration from that point forward. It also changed life for everyone in America. ❋

Opposite: *Chinese Americans in New York's Chinatown gather to read newspapers announcing that the Japanese will surrender at the end of World War II.*

Chapter Four

The Door
Reopens

A New Political Climate

The World at War

On December 7, 1941, Japanese pilots bombed more than 100 American ships that were stationed at Pearl Harbor, Hawaii. World War II (1939–1945) was already raging in Europe, and the Japanese army had been fighting in China for 10 years. The attack on Pearl Harbor brought the United States into World War II.

It's a Fact!

Although Chinese Americans serving in the U.S. armed forces during World War II were not segregated, or separated, from white Americans, as Japanese Americans and African Americans were, they still encountered prejudice. Still, some Chinese Americans were so anxious to serve that they lied about their age.

Suddenly the United States and China had a common enemy, Japan. The Chinese-American community strongly supported the United States's war effort against Japan and its ally Germany.

Some Chinese-American men worked in factories helping to build the weapons of war. Many left low-paying jobs in their Chinatowns and joined America's economic mainstream by filling in for men who had left their jobs to go to war. Once feared and hated, Chinese factory workers were now welcomed as they joined all Americans in the war effort. Chinese-American women also helped. They joined the Women's Army Corps (WACs) and worked in other war-related jobs as well.

Many Chinese Americans gave their lives fighting for the United States. More than 13,000 Chinese Americans fought in World War II. Some Chinese-American boys who were too young to join the army lied about their ages in order to enlist.

At first, some Chinese-American soldiers experienced prejudice from white soldiers. But many things changed once the bullets started flying. Ark Chin, an engineer from Seattle, Washington, recalls what it was like to be a Chinese American in the U.S. Army during World War II:

> *In those days most of the Chinese who were drafted were put in the kitchen. It was stereotyped segregation. They became the cooks. I was thrown into the infantry. I was the only Chinese foot soldier in my company. That experience either makes you or breaks you. That experience for me was transforming. I was wounded twice as an infantryman. Then I went back as a squad leader, and so there were a number of people whose lives I had to look after, besides my own. Once we started to go overseas, heading for action in Europe, all segregation and discrimination disappeared. We were all "buddy-buddy" because we realized that we needed each other, and that I was the most experienced guy there. Everyone realized that my experience was worth something in helping them to survive. I got huge respect from my men, and that was not something that I had experienced before in the United States.*

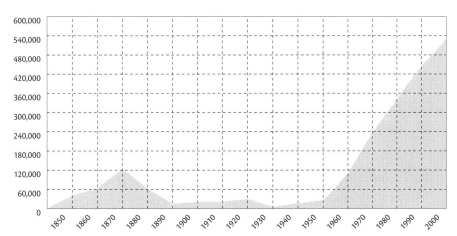

Chinese Immigration to America

As the war against Japan progressed, anti-Japanese feelings grew in the United States. Some Chinese Americans feared being mistaken for Japanese. Chinese-American shop owners put signs in their store windows saying "This shop is Chinese-owned." Some people even wore buttons that read "I am a Chinese."

New stereotypes emerged. Chinese were now said to be "hardworking, honest, and brave." Their facial expressions were described as "kindly and open." Japanese, on the other hand, were said to be "treacherous, cruel, and warlike," and their faces were "arrogant."

Many Americans now had friendly feelings toward the Chinese. The stereotype they chose to believe was now a positive stereotype. Because of the war with Japan, negative stereotypes were used to describe Japanese people in general.

Excellence in Architecture

Ieoh Ming (I. M.) Pei, one of the most famous architects in the world, was born in Guangzhou, China, in 1917. Pei came to the United States in 1935 to study architecture at the University of Pennsylvania. He felt that his architectural drawing ability was not good enough, so he transferred to the Massachusetts Institute of Technology (MIT), where he studied engineering and design. Eventually, he returned to the study of architecture at Harvard University. Pei went to work for an architectural firm and quickly became an expert at designing office buildings and low-cost housing for cities. I. M. Pei designed many famous buildings. These include the Rock and Roll Hall of Fame in Cleveland, Ohio; the John F. Kennedy Memorial Library in Boston; and a bank in Hong Kong that is one of the tallest buildings in Asia.

The design of the Rock and Roll Hall of Fame building in Cleveland, Ohio, shows the creative talents of Chinese architect I. M. Pei.

Chiang Kai-shek

During World War II, the U.S. government gave great amounts of military and financial aid to the government of General Chiang Kai-shek in China. Chiang was the head of the Chinese Nationalist Army, which led the battle against the Japanese. He was also the leader of the Republic of China, the government that had replaced the Manchus when they were overthrown in 1911. General Chiang Kai-shek was popular among Chinese Americans.

In 1943, the general's wife, Meiling Soong, known to the world as Madame Chiang Kai-shek, came to the United States. She hoped to promote friendship between China and the United States and to support both countries' war efforts. She also came to ask for the repeal of the Chinese Exclusion Act.

*Madame Chiang Kai-shek greets guests at a formal reception during
her visit to the United States in 1943.*

Madame Chiang Kai-shek's visit was a huge success.
Thousands of Americans came out to greet her in each city she
visited. Others followed her travels through newspaper stories
and short films, known as newsreels, shown in theaters. (Since
there was no television in 1943, this was the only way people
could see news events.) In Madame Chiang Kai-shek, Americans
saw a woman of great charm and grace. She dressed in stylish
clothing and gave moving, interesting speeches in English. She
quickly became a national hero to many Americans, both those
who were Chinese and those who were not.

Americans' attitudes about the Chinese had changed. The
United States and China were allies in the war. Madame Chiang
Kai-shek promoted a new image of Chinese people. The result
was the repeal of the Chinese Exclusion Act. President Franklin

D. Roosevelt himself urged Congress to do away with the 60-year-old law. He asked Congress "to be big enough to acknowledge our mistakes of the past." He said that lifting the immigration ban would "correct a historic mistake."

Congress quickly passed a bill repealing the Chinese Exclusion Act. The president signed it into law on December 17, 1943.

Postwar Immigration

The biggest change in Chinese immigration in the years after World War II ended in 1945 was the arrival of large numbers of women. Wives of male immigrants were once again allowed to join their husbands. This led to even more Chinese women coming to America than had come in the years from 1910 to 1924, when wives of immigrants were first allowed to join their husbands.

In 1945, Congress passed the War Brides Act. This law allowed

It's a Fact!

During World War II, with anti-Japanese feelings running high in the United States, Chinese American Joseph Chiang, *Time* magazine's Washington correspondent, wore a badge on his jacket that read: "Chinese Reporter—NOT Japanese—Please."

women from Europe and Asia who had married American servicemen while the men were stationed overseas to join their husbands in the United States. The War Brides Act helped about 6,000 more Chinese women to come to the United States.

The repeal of the Chinese Exclusion Act, along with new laws such as the War Brides Act, greatly increased the total number of Chinese immigrants coming to America. By 1950, the Chinese-American population had grown to more than 117,000, up from 77,000 in 1940. This number included 40,000 women.

With the arrival of Chinese women in great numbers, more Chinese Americans were able to enjoy traditional family life. The late 1940s and early 1950s saw the first great Chinese-American "baby boom." (A baby boom is a period of time when more than the usual number of babies are born.) By 1950, almost half of Chinese Americans had been born in the United States. Chinese people began to assimilate (blend) into American society. More and more Chinese Americans began to leave Chinatowns. They moved out into the newly expanding suburbs spreading across the United States.

The Communist Takeover

In 1945, the Japanese surrendered, ending World War II. This surrender also ended nearly two decades of war between Japan and China. No sooner had this conflict ended than China erupted into civil war.

Chinese Communists, led by Mao Zedong, battled against Chiang Kai-shek's Chinese Nationalist Army. In 1949, the Communists defeated the Nationalists and established the People's Republic of China (PRC). The PRC was also called mainland China, Communist China, and Red China. Chiang Kai-shek and his followers fled to the island of Taiwan, just off the coast of China. There they created their own government, known as the Republic of China or Nationalist China.

The United States had supported Chiang Kai-shek during his war with the Japanese. It continued to support him on the island of Taiwan. Likewise, most Chinese Americans still supported Chiang Kai-shek's Nationalist government. And while some Chinese Americans supported Mao and the Communists, the U.S. government refused to recognize Mao Zedong's Chinese government. It did not allow trade or any communications with Communist China. This meant that about 5,000 Chinese students, professionals, and diplomats, who had come to the United States on a temporary basis, could not return to their homes. This political barrier became known as the Bamboo curtain.

Some did not want to return to live in a Communist country. Others feared that they would be punished, put in prison, or even killed if they returned. Many Chinese Americans could not contact their relatives in the PRC. Too afraid to return to China, they often went years with no word from those back home.

The leader of the Chinese Communists, General Mao Zedong, reviews troops in Beijing in 1949 following the retreat of the Chinese Nationalists from the mainland.

The Communist victory in China triggered a wave of
Chinese immigration. Thousands fled the harsh Communist
government. During the first big wave of Chinese immigration
100 years earlier, most of the people who came to the United
States were poor peasants in search of work, gold, and a better
life. The Chinese immigrants who came following the
Communist takeover were mostly wealthy and well educated.
Mao took control of people's personal property and wealth as
part of his Communist philosophy. Those who had property or
money stood to lose the most under Communist rule. For that
reason, they decided to flee to the United States.

Wong Chun Yau was one of the many who left China after
the Communists took over. The Communist government
accused him of crimes against the people. Wong described these
so-called crimes:

> In China, I owned two houses. And if you had money in
> China, it was a crime. If you were an intellectual [educated
> person], it was a crime. The really poor, who didn't have
> anything, they were the average, so no harm came to them. But
> if you had a cent, they would purge [take it from] you. If you
> owned land, they would purge you. They took everything—my
> money, my furniture.

Those who had enjoyed a comfortable life in China now
feared losing everything. Many fled the Communist country for
the freedoms offered in the United States.

Opposite: *Chinese women operate sewing machines in a garment
factory in New York City. They may be among the estimated 50,000
illegal immigrants who work in sweatshops in the New York City area.*

Chapter Five

The Great
Leap Forward

Fleeing to America

Fleeing Famine

In 1958, Mao Zedong introduced a program that he hoped would quickly make China an industrialized nation. Mao hoped to bring modern technology and industry to China. The program was called "The Great Leap Forward."

Under this plan, Mao outlawed private property, including privately run farms. No longer could farmers own land and work their own farms. Instead, they were forced to live and work on large farms owned by the government. Mao demanded that these farmworkers raise an extremely large amount of grain and other crops. He punished the people on the farms that did not meet his unrealistic goals. Rather than face punishment for failing to grow enough crops, many Chinese peasants moved to cities to work in factories.

Soon less and less land was being farmed and China could not produce enough food to feed its large population. A terrible famine

It's a Fact!

Hiram Fong was the first Chinese American to be elected to the U.S. Senate. He was elected in 1959 as a senator from the brand-new state of Hawaii.

followed. (A famine occurs when large numbers of people do not have enough to eat.) Not only was this the worst famine in Chinese history, it was one of the worst in human history. By the early 1960s, between 20 and 30 million people had starved to death in China.

In 1962, the Great Leap Forward was brought to a stop. Mao Zedong himself admitted that it had been a mistake. With his people starving to death, Mao allowed about 70,000 people, mostly from Guangdong province, to leave the country.

Chinese workers are shown drying wheat at the Pauguishen agricultural production center in China in 1962. The average salary for a worker was about $4.00 per day.

Most of these people went to Hong Kong. Hong Kong was a British colony at that time, which meant that it was not under the control of Mao and the Communists. As desperate, hungry people poured into Hong Kong, the city quickly became overcrowded.

New Immigration Laws

In May 1962, President John F. Kennedy signed a law that allowed Chinese refugees who were living in Hong Kong but had been born in the PRC to come to the United States. In the years that followed, more than 15,000 Chinese refugees arrived in America from Hong Kong.

Then, in 1965, President Lyndon Johnson signed the Immigration and Nationality Act. This law eliminated old limits on immigration from all nations. It allowed an equal number of immigrants from every country, including China, into the United States each year. The number of immigrants allowed from each country was 20,000.

The Immigration and Nationality Act of 1965 had a huge impact on the size of the Chinese community in America. In 1960, there were approximately 235,000 Chinese people living in the United States. From the mid-1960s on, the population of Chinese Americans doubled every ten years. Also, for the first time in history, more than half of the Chinese in America were women.

Regardless of what kind of job these new immigrants had held in China or Hong Kong, most started out in the United States at low-paying jobs. Because they could not speak English, many people who were doctors in China worked in laundries or restaurants in the United States. Teachers, accountants, social workers, and newspaper reporters took jobs as busboys, janitors, or messengers.

Amy Tan

Many Americans got their first glimpse into life in a Chinese-American family through the books of Chinese-American writer Amy Tan. Her novels *The Joy Luck Club*, *The Kitchen God's Wife*, and *The Bonesetter's Daughter* introduced many readers to Chinese-American families, especially mother-daughter relationships.

Many newly arriving Chinese worked in factories, making everything from cigars to clothing. Conditions in many Chinatown factories were dangerous. The buildings were over-crowded, too hot or cold, and some did not have enough fire exits for everyone to leave safely in case of a fire.

Chinese women who worked in garment (clothing) factories labored for long hours with no pay for overtime, sick leave, or health benefits. These factories became known as sweatshops because of the overcrowded, hot conditions in which the laborers were forced to work. A Chinese seamstress named Dong Zem recalled her years working at a sewing machine in a garment factory:

> *I can still recall the times when I had one foot on the pedal and another on an improvised rocker, rocking one son to sleep while the other was tied to my back. Many times I would accidentally sew my finger instead of the fabric because one child screamed or because I was falling asleep on the job.*

In addition to sometimes dangerous, low-paying jobs, new Chinese immigrants faced other problems. Conflicts broke out between the American-born Chinese, called ABCs, and the new immigrants, called FOBs (fresh off the boat). Gang violence erupted between teenagers in these groups. As a result, Chinatowns in the 1960s were often dangerous places. The FOBs considered the ABCs to be spoiled and privileged. Since the FOBs lacked English skills, they often failed at school and dropped out. Some took their frustrations out against the better-educated, English-speaking ABCs.

A group called the Chinese for Affirmative Action tried to change one of the root causes of this violence. The group helped Chinese students file a lawsuit against school officials to get the schools to create a bilingual (English and Chinese) education system for newly arriving Chinese students. In 1974, a U.S. Supreme Court ruling opened the door for bilingual education in American schools. This benefited not only Chinese but all non-English-speaking immigrants.

President Nixon strolls across a bridge in Hangzhou (Hang-chou), China, with Chinese foreign minister Zhou Enlai (Chou En-lai) during his historic trip to China in 1972.

The Death of Mao

When Mao Zedong and the Communists took over China in 1949, the United States considered the Nationalists in Taiwan to be the "true" China. By the late 1960s, though, the poor relationship between the United States and the People's Republic of China began to improve.

In February 1972, President Richard Nixon spent eight days in the People's Republic of China. He was the first U.S. president ever to visit China. During his time there, he met with Mao Zedong. The two leaders agreed to open communications between their countries. They hoped that this would lead to future trade and business agreements.

In 1976, Mao Zedong died. He left behind a starving country that was suffering politically and economically. Its farms were ruined, and its technology and industry were not as advanced as those in other countries.

Deng Xiaoping (Teng Hsiao-p'ing) became the new Chinese leader. He went to work immediately to reverse the damage that Mao had done. Deng promoted a capitalist economy, similar to the economy of the United States. He did away with the government farms and allowed farmers to keep their profits rather than force the farmers to give the money to the government. Industry also grew. People were given the chance to start their own businesses.

An Idea That Changed the World

An Wang was born in 1920 in Shanghai, China. In 1945, he came to the United States to study at Harvard University in Massachusetts. Wang watched as the first computer was built there in the 1940s. This original computer was 51 feet (15 m) long, 8 feet (2.4 m) high, and difficult to use. In 1948, while still a student, Wang got an idea for a smaller computer that would be easier to use. In 1951, he started Wang Laboratories. His goal was to create the first word processor, which would combine a computer, video screen, and keyboard. His Wang word processor turned the company into a billion-dollar business. Word processing programs are used by millions of people every day in homes, schools, and workplaces all around the world. They are all based on An Wang's first word processor.

Deng also opened up China to the rest of the world. In 1979, he established a good relationship with the United States. No longer did the two countries think of each other as enemies. These many changes in China would lead to an even greater increase in Chinese immigration to the United States in the coming decade.

Opposite: *A Chinese-American mother watches her two daughters rush off to catch the school bus.*

Chapter Six

Lifting the Bamboo Curtain

Becoming More American

The Rules Change

In the early 1980s, U.S. president Ronald Reagan and Chinese leader Deng Xiaoping signed historic agreements that increased trade and the sharing of cultural, technological, and scientific information between the two nations. Chinese immigration rules were also changed.

Since 1965, under the Immigration and Nationality Act, 20,000 Chinese immigrants were allowed into the United States each year. Most came from Taiwan. Once a good relationship was established between the United States and the mainland Chinese government in 1979, another 20,000 people were allowed to emigrate from the mainland each year. By the late 1980s, an additional 5,000 people were allowed to come from Hong Kong, which was still controlled by the British.

*Most Chinese immigrants have settled
in these states.*

In addition to the 45,000 Chinese immigrants allowed each year, Chinese visitors such as students, government officials, and tourists were allowed into the United States. Many stayed once they were in the United States.

The Model Minority

E ducation was always very important to Chinese Americans. Life in the Chinese community was strongly influenced by the teachings of Confucius, which stressed hard work, self-help, thrift, respect for others, and education.

In 1980, 47 percent of Chinese-American men and 33 percent of Chinese-American women between the ages of 25 and 64 had completed at least four years of college. This compared to 22 percent of men and 14 percent of women among white Americans. As a group, Chinese Americans tended to outperform the general student population, especially in science and math.

The achievements of Chinese Americans in education, along with other cultural traits, led some Americans in the 1980s to view the Chinese as a "model minority." This meant that the Chinese were viewed as a minority immigrant group who had the ability to succeed in America. They were hardworking and likely to save money rather than fall into debt. They often

It's a Fact!

Maya Yang Lin was a 21-year-old architecture student at Yale University in Connecticut when her design was selected for the Vietnam Veterans Memorial in Washington, D.C., in 1981. Her design had competed against the nearly 1,400 others considered for the memorial. In 1989, she was asked to design a memorial for the American civil rights movement. This memorial now stands in Montgomery, Alabama.

turned to family members or Chinese associations in times of need, rather than to government-sponsored assistance programs such as welfare.

The "model minority" label was meant to be a compliment. But it was actually a kind of stereotyping. This label put a great deal of pressure on Chinese-American students. High, if not perfect, test scores were expected of them. Students were also expected to excel at playing a musical instrument. Chinese-American parents' desire to have their children attend top colleges led to family conflicts. Even so, large numbers of successful Chinese-American students graduated from America's best universities. Many of these graduates became doctors or engineers.

Small lights in the ground illuminate the Wall of the Vietnam Veterans Memorial in Washington, D.C. The memorial was designed by Chinese-American architectural student Maya Yang Lin.

When they completed their educations, many Chinese Americans found good jobs and chose to leave the Chinatowns in which they had grown up. They moved into the mainstream American middle class, living and working among Americans of all backgrounds. By the early 1990s, fewer than half of all Chinese Americans lived in Chinatowns. Even so, Chinatowns continued to thrive. New immigrants felt most comfortable there, and tourists continued to visit in large numbers.

Expanding Horizons

As they moved out of Chinatowns, Chinese Americans also moved away from traditional Chinese culture and into the mainstream American culture. Chinese families began facing many changes.

For example, single-parent families and divorce, once unheard-of in traditional Chinese families, are on the rise among younger Chinese Americans. Marriage between Chinese and non-Chinese people also became more common. These are big changes from traditional Chinese culture.

Chinese people began to give their children American first names. Also, traditional Chinese names were

It's a Fact!

Chinese-American tennis player Michael Chang became the youngest man ever to win the French Open, one of the top tournaments in professional tennis. Chang captured the title in 1989 at the age of 17.

sometimes reversed so that the family name came last, as with American names. For example, the famous cellist Yo-Yo Ma's family name is Ma. When he introduces himself in Chinese he calls himself "Ma Yo-Yo."

Tension between parents born in another country and their children, born and raised in America, is a common part of every

Jackie Chan

Jackie Chan was born in Hong Kong in 1954. His real name is Chan Kong-san. At the age of seven, he became a student at the China Drama Academy. There he learned mime, dance, acrobatics, and martial arts. He has incorporated all of these elements into his popular action films. After working with legendary Chinese martial arts expert Bruce Lee on several of Lee's films, Chan set out on his own. He quickly became Asia's highest paid film actor. In 1995, Chan went to Hollywood, where he has starred in such action hits as *Rush Hour* and *Shanghai Noon*. He has always done his own stunts, no matter how dangerous. Chan is now an actor, director, producer, writer, and stuntman of great influence in the world of action movies.

immigrant group's story. This was no different for the Chinese. Chinese-American parents often insisted that their children follow traditional customs and have traditional values. The children, on the other hand, viewed themselves as Americans and wanted the freedom to make their own choices. These choices were often based on what they saw among their non-Chinese peers.

But even as Chinese Americans blended into mainstream American society, prejudice, in the form of nativism, raised its ugly head once again. Nativism, the belief that native-born people should be favored over immigrants, flared up during the economic difficulties of the 1990s. As in the tough times of the 1870s, in the 1990s those who considered themselves "real" Americans were quick to blame immigrants, such as the Chinese. On college campuses, nativism produced anger toward Chinese (and other Asian) students, as competition among those training for fewer and fewer jobs grew fierce.

Excellence in Music

Yo-Yo Ma is a famous musician who plays the cello, a stringed instrument. He is one of the finest musicians in the world. His father, Ma Hiao-Tsium, was a professor of music at Nanjing University in China. In 1936, Hiao-Tsium went to Paris, France, to study music. He ended up staying there for many years. In 1955, Yo-Yo Ma was born in Paris. The family moved to New York City in 1962, where Hiao-Tsium started the Children's Orchestra of New York. Yo-Yo Ma studied music all his life. He played in his first concert at the age of five. When he was old enough, he attended the Juilliard School of Music, one of the best music schools in the United States.

Being Chinese but living in the United States, Yo-Yo Ma often felt caught between two worlds. At school, his teachers encouraged him to express his individuality. At home, he was taught never to talk back to his parents. Chinese was the only language spoken in his home. Today Yo-Yo Ma is proud of both his Chinese and American culture.

Tiananmen Square

By 1989, ten years after the United States recognized the People's Republic of China, students in Beijing began demanding change. They wanted more democracy in China. The students staged street parades and demonstrations. In May 1989, approximately 100,000 students gathered in Beijing for a huge pro-democracy demonstration in a large open plaza called Tiananmen Square.

Deng Xiaoping decided that this democracy movement had to be stopped. In early June, he sent out the Chinese army to break up the demonstration. More than 2,600 people were killed and more than 10,000 were injured. The leaders of the pro-democracy movement were rounded up and arrested.

*An ambulance stands ready to transport hunger strikers to a hospital
during the Tiananmen Square protests of May 1989.*

After this event, Chinese immigration increased. About
32,000 students who were in the United States decided not to
go back to China. They feared they might be punished or
killed if they returned. In 1992, the United States passed the
Chinese Student Protection Act, which allowed more than
50,000 Chinese students to become permanent residents of the
United States.

The terrible events in Tiananmen Square caused fear and
worry among Chinese people on the mainland, in Taiwan, and in

Hong Kong. Seeing the violence that Deng Xiaoping had used to stop Chinese people when they demanded more freedom, many in mainland China left for the freedom offered in the United States. Those in Taiwan feared Deng Xiaoping because they had a democratic society. They were afraid that Deng would use his military might to take control of the island. Hong Kong, which had been ruled by the British for nearly 150 years, was scheduled to become part of the People's Republic of China in 1997. The citizens of Hong Kong knew that, in a matter of years, they would be under the control of Deng Xiaoping's government. Fearing this change, many residents of Hong Kong came to the United States.

The Dot-Com Boom

The growth of the Internet in the 1990s, a period known as the "dot-com boom," led to a wave of Chinese immigrants with skills in computer science. Like the first Chinese immigrants who went to California for the gold rush, those who arrived during the dot-com boom brought with them dreams of quick riches in America.

Those who had the high-tech skills needed by the Internet industry settled in an area south of San Francisco known as Silicon Valley. It had been named for the silicon chips that make computers work. Many dot-coms, or companies that were Internet-based, were very successful very quickly. Because of this success, many young Chinese immigrants, who had the right high-tech skills, became millionaires in a matter of months in the 1990s.

At the same time, unskilled Chinese immigrants continued to pour into the United States. Most of these new arrivals worked long hours for low pay in poor conditions in sweatshops in Chinatowns throughout the United States.

Yahoo!

Jerry Yang, the creator and founder of Yahoo!, was born in Taiwan in 1967. He emigrated with his family to San Jose, California, when he was a teenager. Yang's idea for an Internet search engine that helps people find what they are looking for on the World Wide Web came out of a list he made of his own favorite Web sites. He believed that other people might want to easily find the sites they were interested in. At the age of 26, Yang was a doctoral student in electrical engineering at Stanford University in California. Working in a tiny office at the university, he developed the first search engine for the Internet. Yahoo!, as he called it, was the first software that showed people all the sites related to the subject they were interested in. So many people used Yahoo! at first that the university's computers crashed. Yang moved off campus and started his business. Jerry Yang helped Yahoo! grow into one of the Internet's most successful companies.

The Littlest Immigrants

Overpopulation in China led to a new kind of Chinese immigrant in America. By 1979, China's population had grown too large for the country's resources. There simply was not enough food to feed everyone. In response, China started a "one-child family" policy. In this program, couples who had only one child received government benefits. Those that had more than one child had to pay high penalties.

In Chinese tradition, it was very important for a family to have a son. This would ensure that the family name would continue to the next generation. Many Chinese couples hoped that their one child would be a boy. If their child was a girl, they often abandoned the baby. The couple then hoped that their next child would be a boy.

Newborn baby girls in China were often left at police stations, public parks, on the doorsteps of orphanages, or even on the side of the road. Orphanages were overwhelmed with this new population of homeless baby girls. When people in the United States learned what was happening in China, many American families began adopting the babies. The process for Americans to adopt a Chinese baby was long and complicated. Hopeful parents often had to wait up to a year to get their baby. When it was time to bring their baby home, the American parents would fly to China to meet their new daughter.

An American woman holds her newly adopted daughter soon after meeting her for the first time in Guangzhou, China.

Deborah Sullivan of New York City is a single parent of a Chinese girl she adopted and named Nina (the girl was named Fu Xin Xuan by the orphanage where she spent the first 16 months of her life). Sullivan describes what it was like to adopt her daughter from China:

I did some research on the internet and learned a lot about Chinese adoption, and the whole story of little Chinese girls being abandoned by their families because of the Chinese government's one-child policy. . . . The little girls are just left at police stations, orphanages, or in busy marketplaces.

I had to find an agency that does Chinese adoptions, then I had to gather a lot of paperwork. . . . It took about five months to get all the paperwork together. I then waited another 14 months while all the paperwork was processed in China before I got the okay to go get her. Then I was sent her referral, which included a picture and a little medical evaluation. It also had additional information about what kind of kid she was, which actually turned out to be fairly true to who she is.

Then I traveled to China with a friend to get her. We traveled in a group of other families all from the same agency going to China to get their babies. . . . [We] traveled to [the city of] Chuzhou to a big hotel. In the hotel's conference room they had all the babies. We were all standing in the doorway looking at our new babies, crying. Then, one by one, they called us in and gave the babies to us.

We then went to Guangdong province, where we stayed for three days while her immigration papers were processed by the U.S. embassy. Then I could finally bring Nina home, where she's been very happy living in New York.

As the daughters of American citizens, these babies are also American citizens. Although they were raised in the United States, these smallest of Chinese immigrants often express curiosity about their ethnic heritage once they are old enough to realize their situation. Many American parents of Chinese babies do their best to teach their children about the land in which the children were born. Just like other Chinese immigrants, who came to America seeking a better life, these children have become a unique part of American culture.

Today in Chinese communities, holidays are still celebrated as they have been for decades. Big parades and fireworks still fill the streets during the Chinese New Year. Families still gather to remember relatives that are gone, and children still learn the importance of their Chinese heritage. But Chinese culture in America is not only for Chinese Americans. For more than a century and a half, Chinese immigrants have been coming to the United States. Through the innovations these immigrants brought, and the struggles and successes they have experienced, many aspects of Chinese culture, from food to holiday celebrations, have become part of the fabric of life in America for people of all backgrounds.

Time Line of Chinese Immigration

1644   Manchu dynasty takes control of China.

1848   Gold is discovered in California. Many Chinese begin journey to Gold Mountain in search of wealth.

1862   Work on the transcontinental railroad begins. Many Chinese are hired as workers. Chinatowns spread to many cities around the United States.

1868   Burlingame Treaty allows unrestricted Chinese immigration. During the next twelve years, the Chinese population in the United States triples.

1882   Chinese Exclusion Act greatly restricts Chinese immigration for a limited period.

1888   Scott Act bars even legal Chinese immigrants from reentering the United States once they leave.

1904   Chinese Exclusion Act is continued indefinitely.

1906   San Francisco earthquake and fire destroy birth and death records. Many Chinese immigrants arrive, claiming to be American-born.

1910   Angel Island opens. Chinese immigrants are held there, often for months, under terrible conditions.

1924   Immigration Act of 1924 prohibits most Chinese women from entering the United States.

1931   Japan invades China.

1941   Japan bombs Pearl Harbor. The United States enters World War II and the United States and China become allies against Japan.

1943	The ban on Chinese immigration is lifted.
1949	Communists, led by Mao Zedong take over China, naming it the People's Republic of China (PRC). Nationalists, led by Chiang Kai-shek, flee to the island of Taiwan. Rich and well-educated Chinese citizens flee Mao's regime.

1950s	First Chinese-American baby boom. Chinese families begin to move out of Chinatowns and into suburbs.
1962	President John F. Kennedy allows refugees in Hong Kong who were born in the PRC to come to the United States.
1965	President Lyndon Johnson signs the Immigration and Nationality Act.
1972	President Richard Nixon becomes the first U.S. president to visit China.
1976	Mao Zedong dies.
1977	Deng Xiaoping becomes China's leader.

1979	Trade opens up between the United States and China, and relations improve greatly.
1980s	The new open relationship between the United States and China triggers the third great wave of Chinese immigration to the United States.
1990s	The dot-com boom of the 1990s brings many Chinese immigrants with high-tech skills to California.
2000	Chinese American Gary Locke, the first Asian-American governor in the United States, is elected to a second term in Washington State.
2001	Elaine Chao is named secretary of labor in President George W. Bush's cabinet. She is the first Chinese American to be appointed to a cabinet position.
2003	*Hyphen*, a magazine aimed at young Asian Americans, is launched in San Francisco.

Glossary

assimilate Absorb or blend into the way of life of a society.

culture The language, arts, traditions, and beliefs of a society.

democracy Government by the majority rule of the people.

dynasty Powerful group or family that rules a nation for a long time.

emigrate Leave one's homeland to live in another country.

entrepreneur Person who starts a business.

ethnic Having certain racial, national, tribal, religious, or cultural origins.

exclusion Keeping one ethnic or national group from entering a country.

famine Shortage of food; extended period of widespread hunger.

immigrate Come to a foreign country to live.

nativism Prejudice in favor of people born in a nation and against immigrants who settle in that nation.

opium Addictive drug made from poppies.

pinyin A system of translating the characters of the Chinese written language into other languages.

prejudice Negative opinion formed without just cause.

racism Belief that one race is better than others.

refugee Someone who flees a place for safety reasons, especially to another country.

queue A long braid of hair worn by Chinese men.

stereotype Simplified and sometimes insulting opinion or image of a person or group.

transcontinental Stretching across the entire continent.

Further Reading

BOOKS

Bandon, Alexandra. *Chinese Americans.* Footsteps to America. New York: Macmillan, 1994.

Hoobler, Dorothy and Thomas. *The Chinese American Family Album.* New York: Oxford University Press, 1994.

Martin, Michael. *Chinese Americans.* New York: Chelsea House, 2003.

Olson, Kay Melchisedach. *Chinese Immigrants, 1850–1900.* Mankato, Minn.: Capstone Press, 2001.

Wu, Dana Ying-Hui, and Jeffrey Dao-Sheng Tung. *Coming to America: The Chinese-American Experience.* Brookfield, Conn: Millbrook Press, 1993.

WEB SITES

The Brown Quarterly. "The History of Chinese Immigration." URL: http://www.brownvboard.org/brwnqurt/03-4/03-4c.htm. Updated on May 28, 2000.

The Library of Congress Learning Page. "Rise of Industrial America, 1876–1900: Chinese Immigration to the United States, 1851–1900." URL: http://www.memory.loc.gov/learn/features/timeline/riseind/chinimms/chinimms.html. Updated on February 3, 2004.

The National Park Service ParkNet. "A History of Chinese Americans in California." URL: http://www.cr.nps.gov/history/onlinebooks/5views/5views3.htm. Downloaded on June 1, 2004.

Index